# Poetic Chronicles

**By Jazz Matazz**
**aka**
**Jeffrey E. Jones**

F.C.E. PUBLISHING

## Cover design by Ricky S. Holmes

**ISBN 13- 9780615464633**

Library of Congress Cataloging in Publication Data
Jeffrey E. Jones aka Jazz Matazz
Poetic Chronicles
Library of Congress Control Number: 2011939289

Edited by: Theresa Gonsalves, Patricia Hoover, & Natasha Hughes

Published by FCE Publishing, Las Vegas, Nv.
All Publishing Rights – Second printing 2024

# Contents

# THE INTRODUCTION

People never seem to see me as a poet at first glance. I've been told because I am such a *manly type*, I appear least likely to pen verses about things I am most passionate about.

I tell them, the people, that my journey and love affair with poetry and words came at an early age; I can, however, remember it, like it was yesterday.

I was in the fifth grade in Miss Segal's class when she asked the students to write poems. I wrote about the color blue. I didn't know if it made sense to anyone else, but it made perfect sense to me. I was proud of that piece and found myself penning various short stories to pass the long hours in school. I have had the poetry bug ever since and I can still remember the entire poem titled Blue:

*Blue*

*Blue is Mars a fruit*
 *to chew*
*I love Blue and it loves me*
*too*

*If Blue were my name*
*I would not be ashamed*
*I would just be the same*
*Loving Blue*

# PROLOGUE

*In 2006, God blessed me to pen and publish my first book, Poetic Voices, which was inspired by a collection of poems that I had written over a period of several years. This book, Poetic Chronicles, speaks to the life and times of day-to-day living as we have come to know it, along with snapshots of conversations that were inspiring enough to pen verses to.*

*The Memories of our ancestors, the stressors of everyday living and the joys of ushering in the first Black President are all recorded in this book.*

## The Genius of Poetry

Met this genius when I was just ten
Over time became fond
And soon much more than friends

Tagged along every place she would go
Spoken words, scraps of paper strung along by
her flow
Simply felt her like that cause she made my thang
grow

Still I knew that some might misconstrue
This new Jones, for my love, I began to pursue
She would bug me til' I'd do her right
Metaphoric concepts schemed until they were
tight

And as thoughts of her raced through my mind
Gathered pencil and paper and began to combine
A few phrases in stanzas that would quite often
rhyme

She'd appear in the strangest of places
Mystic messages, accompanied by flowers in
vases
Though she'd share every thought, deepest secrets
were kept
Told those inner most whispers that folks read as
they wept

And she'd scribed some that proved more than
tricky
Stimulating Haikus that were penned in a quickie

With an unselfish nature that would to speak to us
all
She got lost more than once wasn't saved or
recalled
Sonnets love affairs; built to seduce from the start
Styles and rhythms enticing, introduced me to art
Heard my cry when the world didn't notice me
Fell in love with the genius of poetry.

## Word Choice

My Choice of Words may not be right
But I do help to shed some light
As I speak thoughts from many heads
Quite frankly things that go unsaid
You must agree that most conceal
Their naked selves despite how real
Truth is most truths comes from the heart
And may seem harsh but that's a part
That some want badly to control
So few do bare an exposed soul
Been said, "the truth will set you free"
Still many a man may not agree
I know my word choice might be flawed
But said and done I'm not the fraud.

**Better off Read**

What happened to all the Poetic Thoughts poets?
They've got something to say and I think we all
know it.

There's such moving about at this time, in this life
But where are all the rhymes about family and
strife?

The Presidential Politricks and other deceit
The similes and rhythms about the ways people
cheat

Those metaphors of love might be just the
technique
To evoke inspiration
I believe we all seek!

Have you lowered your pens and begun to
concede
Or just vowed not to write even though there's a
need?

With the terror of hurricanes like Gustav and Ike
I have heard not a word, are you poets on strike?

Overstand through your verses that many take
note
That you think of these concepts that may become
quotes

Is it hard to believe that at times you inspire
A few lines in the minds many others admire

So I ask all you poets if you've thoughts in your heads
Overstand that your thoughts will be better off read!

**If I had to tell the Truth**

If I had to tell the truth
I'd change my clothes inside a phone booth
And save this world from its demise
Pray folks would open up their eyes
And Stop believing their own lies

If I had to tell the Truth
I'd make my way to droves of youth
I'd tell them all to hold life tight
Respect their elders and be polite
I'd tell them shoot for the Moon & Stars
Cuz we're not all built for sixteen bars
And since young egos tend to scar
I 'd say to them "be who you are."

Because IT IS not what IT IS
And I am far from being a wiz
Truth is we all should know the biz
And cherish life for what it gives
Let's overstand that breath is crucial
The very basis of living fruitful
In times of witnessing more of less
And age-old kinships put to rest
Over straight up Cow Chips mixed with mess
Keep bended knees, make prayer requests.

If I had to tell the Truth
You'd know some Christians drank that hooch
May know bout' Joshua, Judges, & Ruth
But can't turn loose them vice pursuits
So If I had to tell the Truth

There wouldn't be no mysteries for sleuths
Folks might be nursing shrapnel wounds
From rapid fired facts consumed
And if I had to tell the Truth
I'd out the Governments in cahoots

Send them to Court on Truth lawsuits

And then I'd give 'em all the boot
No needs for psychics reading minds
There would be no blames or lies assigned
Because I'd Truth yawl by design
Convinced the Truth would leave us fine

See, if I had to tell the Truth
Might find me screaming it from your roof
While trying to capture your attention
Because Truth be told, nobody listens
When it's straight up with out no chaser
Most folks would have you-call- back-later
Or put the word out "you're a hater!"
Instead of becoming a known embracer
That's known for taking it on the chin
Receiving messages from good friends
They knew that never would intend
To tell a Truth meant to offend

## The Stress Piece

Throughout this journey I've felt the stress

And Lord knows my life's been blessed

But lately, something grabbed a hold

Got my mind tied up, and my soul turn'n cold

Still, I can't allow this to take over my being

For I haven't been sowing what I have been
reaping.

In this absence of tranquility

I've questioned mere stability

Reminiscent raw thoughts that are taunted with
wrong

Invite struggles with dark deeds that have proven
too strong

And I've done all I can avoiding slippery slopes

But the harder I try, it seems harder to cope

Because I'm still aware of the easy ways out

Feel'n like I'm just short of going that route

I have carried this weight that felt so much like
boulders

And gone deaf from my screams for relief of these shoulders

And still I hung in as I found myself toting

Some 23rd Psalm that I found myself quoting

For this load that I 've carried proved to be so complex

I' m still bracing myself for whatever comes next!

Growing weaker but stronger through my merciless travels

But send praises on high that I've not come unraveled.

Amen!

**no spare change**

Now I'm down for whoever, but what's going on
Seems like everyone is on some type of  con
That they try to down play and use me as the
pawn.

It's one crazy world, folks forever runn'n game
And some of these are my kins and my friends
At least that what they claim.

Got the nerves to get buck, when I launch my
conflict?
Cause I came with a counter that they didn't
predict?

Still trying to get over, leaving me in disgust
While inflicting infections of such splattered
distrust.

Though I'm down for whoever, I aint with all that
mess
Cause some gimmicks and capers do result in
arrests

And my gut let's me know so I don't have to
guess.
So don't come around here putt'n me to the test

Like a ride up this street, a couple dollars til then
While they're plott'n and scheming, I just let 'em
pretend

As they're lurking, I'm looking; and I check for
God's favor
Though I know we get weak and at times we may
waiver

Still, it is what it is and I know that's cliché
But I'm sick of these vultures seeing me as their
prey

Try'n to hustle on *this* then be plott'n on *that*
Then become aggravated when I turn them down
*flat?*

And some blame paranoia or suggest I seek prayer
When I say they've conspired to catch me off my
square.

Though I see the plots thicken, I still look for
what's real
And I don't hesitate to buy strangers a meal

But don't get *agitated* when I say you've
concealed
That Jones from the fiend that you *failed* to reveal

See, it's not that your vice deems you wicked or
strange
But I'm raising a Child, I don't have no spare
change!!!

**The air I breathe**

The air I breath

aint always fresh

not always crisp and

doesn't always smell clean

sometimes its

polluted,

even toxic...

like you wouldn't believe

And I try but

but try as I might,

I don't always make due

in fact, there are times

that I get under my own skin

breathing in

The air I breathe

cuz it

muddies the very waters of

real and true life

and at times causes me

to play

to play like a

guitar

the soothing smooth sounds of

"whyalwaysme?"

See, the air that I breathe

can be somewhat septic

and does not allow me

to see your trees for my forest...

even when that's my quest

The air I breathe

sometimes causes too much

truth to gush out

spilling over into

the hills of the heedless

and at times even the needless

get a whiff of the air I breathe

so real happens anyway


The air I breathe

gets into my blood stream

and won't allow me

to function

in dysfunction

despite my dysfunction

its just my malfunction

to breathe

the air I breathe.

## I've Been Provoked

Sometimes I want to fly away
Leave my troubles behind; become a stray
And part from this ole scandalous world
Then I think about wifey and our little girl

But Lawd knows I need room to breathe
Step away from this grind though I've made
plenty cheese
Cause today it's just not stretch'n
Feel like teaching these executives a lesson

On the climate of the economy
So I can get back where I want to be
Cause they're going through all my change
Got me headed towards the closet to get that
thang

Then on to Joe's bar to yell "stick em up!"
"Get undressed and put all the money in this here
cup!"

"And don't yall try nothing funny"
Nawl, "It's not fair, but them executives got me
for all my money"

"So unlike the Big Three I'm bailing myself out!"
"You too Pastor cause even you aint devout"
"Over there sipp'n on a malt liquor stout"
"See I'm taking out frustrations"
"Cause I read the publications"
"Indicating that we're all broke"
"Stop your smiling chump this aint no joke
And don't entertain this as a gag or a hoax
Put it this way folks... I've already been
provoked!"

## Sunshine

I need a ray of sunshine; big picture show your
face

Deliverance from the skeptical, without leaving a
trace

I need the courage to believe in life and take it as
it comes

The diligence engrained in me so that I don't
succumb

And If I stumble just a little bit, give me the nerve
to improvise

To persevere throughout the year if it takes a
trillion tries

I need to think in the affirmative; a can do state of
mind

Then overhaul my phobias so that I'm not inclined

To be uncertain and so critical that my blessings
become blocked

To fill my heart with peace and love until it's
overstocked

I want to shoot straight for the moon each time,
do battle with the stars

To charge life at the speed of light regardless of
my scars

I need the pessimistic part of me to be wiped out
today

So that the burst of sunny rays eclipsed will pour
sunshine my way.

**The Tree**

Such inspirational thoughts come from an aging
tree
Even if it reeks a stench, of a shameful history

If each tree could talk, what tales would they all
tell
What secrets would be whispered or mysteries
would dwell
What deeds would we hear spoken, that have
never come to light
What testimonies stifled that folks dare not recite
What paths would we find taken amongst the
grassiest range
What plans would end abruptly, or aspirations
changed

If a tree could tell a story would humanity laugh
or cry
If a tree performed a miracle what odds would it
defy
Would light be thrust upon the land and turn the
heavens gold
If a tree gave such conviction would mankind
then behold
The art of such a simple shrub yet destined to
reply
To questions of a history that begs to question
why.

## Block'n My Dreams

This life for me has been one big hoax
Try'n my best to gain respect from these
folks
But believe me, I know better
And can't follow old blueprints to the
letter

Cause life *as* me "Aint been no crystal
stair"
So nawl, yawl better not even dare
To act as though it has been
Took *hard knock* lessons on my chin

Because that's how it's been dealt to me
Continued struggles to the umteenth
degree
Since Mr. Charlie proclaimed that we's be
free?

Discrimination because of my skin!
Same thing my grand dad had to contend
My patience stretched and way too thin

Cause I'm here, still fight'n everyday
And just like my ancestors refuse to obey
Subliminal messages they're still try'n
convey

So much so that I've written rhymes
Refrained from bloodshed many a time
For fear they'd charge me with a crime

For the ways I'd deal with this uphill climb

For the things that I have had to defend
against
Things I had to pretend convinced I had
never even seen
And its sad, but contempt Still proves
routine
Got the nerves to ask Why I look so mean
But for four hundred years
You've tried block'n my dreams!

## Crumbling Haitian Dreams

We just kept going as a nation
And viewed this crumbling as inflation

Behold, "the stingy generation"
Who dare not mourn our fallen Haitians

You see, my tongue could not be tamed
Amongst the lives the rubble claimed

Affirmed the hunger that was felt
Lost limbs and cards that they 'd been dealt

Disease of each and every kind
Another trying but still confined

Too weak to move another stone
Displaced from families and their homes

A nation bought and sold at birth
Afflicted more by crumbling earth

Though in the distance heard their screams
A host of crumbling Haitian dreams.

# State Of Emergency

We're in a state of Emergency
Can't you smell the urgency?
Of a country in combustion, a nation try'n to
overstand
Why the financial infrastructure underlooked a
fiscal plan

Now Retirements in jeopardy, still my bills keep
piling high
All the grocery stores I frequent Re-priced food
too *sky* to buy
My neighbor's house is in foreclosure, an unpaid
mortgage *swiped* his pride
Meanwhile prices at the gas pumps, got me try'n
to *hitch* a ride

And I'm seeing families suffer, some can barely
cop a meal
A Seven Hundred Billion Bailout can't get passed
on Capitol Hill?
Congress had to see this coming, *tripp'n* kept
things on the low
Through threats of "President" Mc Cain and
bringing back that old Jim Crow

Man, I cram to understand, the whole thing got
me so perplexed
Spend much more time down on my knees as I
thumb through religious texts

Cause I see my states of emergency, Townsfolk
been mubbl'n bout insurgency...
Which makes my thoughts of ever banking mostly
mixed
Because I just want my states Emergency to be
Fixed!

## The Day of Our Reckoning

On the day of our reckoning I'll awake from my
sleep
Read results from the paper, tears of joy I may
weep

I'll rejoice and attest that the people weren't
swayed
When all votes have been counted and the thanks
has been prayed

I may call into work; tell the boss I'm E-ffected
Sounding drunk with emotion, when Barack gets
elected

I may do the moonwalk once they tally the score
And give thanks for this history
then I'll moonwalk some more

Yeah, I'll dance in the streets do the cha cha and
slide
Drink champagne all day long once the people
decide

I may join up with church or take up violin
Just to step up my game once Obama gets in

I may move back down south and buy acres of
land
Pursue higher degrees when Obama's the man

It's a dream for us all that must not be betrayed
And the day of our reckoning which deserves a
parade!

# Change 2008

My Emotions all over the place
Tears running down my face
For a new day has dawned
And without thinking, I find I'm drawn.
To this essence of such history
Obama's place in life was meant to be


Allowing freedom to simply ring
Reminiscent thoughts of Dr. King
Flowing throughout this great land
And not just because he's a black man
Who had us chanting, "Yes we can!"


Brotha Obama Commands attention
A leader who takes the time to listen
You see, so many more dimensions
To this, his, Presidential Cause
And I'm not saying he has no flaws


But he has won a country's heart
Like you I'm proud to be a part
Of such a cherished pivotal time
When one whole nation stood in line
To render a rarity some among us deem as strange
But then, like **President** Obama, we all sought
change!

**I've Got Big Dreams!**

I've Got Big Dreams!
So I'm gone fly'n and spread'n these wings.

Going to shoot for the stars.
And Keep Drive'n "New Cars"
Just like Bob Barker said...
Because I'm grateful not dead
Buy up these houses and some land
Because 4sho I overstand

That I'm supposed to be enjoying this.
And when I'm too old to go maybe reminisce
About which coast I liked best
Whether Ivory or Key West

Meanwhile I'm doing THIS damn thang!
That sounds a lot more colorful when I add that lil
slang
As I'm duck'n and dodge'n those old regimes
Without calculating who'll rein supreme

Just taking time out 2 let MY life flow
Adding food 2 these thoughts, maybe then I can
grow
Could be over tomorrow if yawl didn't already
know

See, my dreams and my hopes weighed in over a
ton
And that's the heaviest reason that I'm living this
one

I've Got Big Dreams!

# Overstanding "Love"

Momma told me there would be days like this

Days when everything seemed somewhat amiss

Times I'd feel challenged by the ones closest

Ones with watered down character shrinkage
through bitchassness osmosis

And I witnessed that today

Smiling in my face like everything was okay

While I'm dealing with this nonsense

Deflecting this ignorance

Manifested through this arrogance

And it's a muthafuck'n shame

Show'n "love" to these phonies that have proven
too lame

To overstand the concept of "love" being an
action word

Look'n upside my head like what I feel is absurd

When nothing could be further from the truth

Feel like I want to square-up, maybe knock out a
tooth

But then that might prove detrimental

And in the end consequential

Man, I've got too much potential

Extreme focus is essential

To the moves that I'm making

And the trees that I'm shaking

Trying to get to higher ground

Find I'm chanting to myself hoping peace will be found

Engaged in heavy consultation with the man up above

So I can underlook these actions and start overstanding "love."

## Loyalty

Is loyalty now overrated?
And simple values antiquated
So many disregard disgust
That follows with betrayals of trust

Consumed by less important things
When loyalties attached with strings
Such damage done and rocks been thrown
By hiding hands we've always known

The jealousy and envy flow
When better men begin to grow
But history should show and prove
That loyalty is still the move.

## COMPANY

Company is cool
But do we have to speak cotton
When our language is really Steel

Company, essential when it comes to trade secrets,
Catching up and becoming acquainted.

But what happens when we stop enjoying company
Because there is too much B.S. in that Mix

We dare not go along to get along
Truth be told we were never really crazy
About the company from the jump.

**Rumor Mill**

Rumor spreading
Conversations
Subgroups meetings
Delegation
Implementation
Seen as confrontation
No inclination
But rationalization
Created animation
Full-blown frustration
This combination
Without investigation
Plus disorganization
Affirmed expectations
Of the reservations
Of manifestation
Created by the rumor mill.

## The Cell Phone is the Devil

The Cell Phone is the devil, yep,
That's how we all should view it
A walking-mobile-voicemail
and please don't misconstrue it

Folks call & talk & talk some more
When nothing really matters
But then, when in essential times,
They isolate the chatter

By texting when they know that
"we" would rather hear a voice
Avoiding pitch and diction while they
Leave "us" without a choice

They won't take those important calls
From people they may owe.
And some ignore their loved ones
Simply calling and wanting to show (show love)

And what of all those risky ones
Who text us as they drive
Making random checks for messages
While believing they'll survive

What about the KEY they say
Communication has always been
The times we need to just drop it all
To chat with our family or a friend?

The Cell phone is the devil, yep
I stand convinced it's true
So don't ignore me, text me, or send me to
voicemail,
I'd rather speak directly to you!

**Natural**

They think they know
But they don't
They think that it's about what it's not
most don't have the guts to be  themselves
An old friend once said
"Be yourself or find yourself by yourself."
I've thrived on being myself and yet for the most
part found  myself  by myself
Because most don't have the guts to be themselves
Even when self preservation
Is the first law of nature
Guess it just doesn't come natural for many.

**Listen to the Bass**

Listen;

Can't you hear the slap and thump of that bass?

That deep melodic soulful sound giving chase

To a melancholy memory

Syncopation with no symphony

Like new-age rhythms spiked with colorful
traditions

Strums that stream negotiable positions

or accompaniments

Soothed by the timely tones of that bass

For every string on this rack has its time in this
space

Mellow mahogany moods beckoning to be
plucked and tried

Eyes and ears open quite wide as most try to
decide

Which lick struck them most from the vibrant
voice of that divine Double Bass.

## A Bucket Full Of Happiness

I want some Jellybeans
Some hopscotch in my life
A bicycle ride down hill
Fresh Red and yellow Tulips
Or a merry-go-round on horseback
A giggle with my grandma,
Twelve helium filled balloons
A breeze amongst the trees
I want slow baby bouncies
Then A bag of cotton candy
I want primary colors
And then I want a bucket
A bucket full of happiness
Freshly picked from being glad.

## I Never Knew

I never knew what joy she'd bring
I never knew the half
The dance moves and the songs she sings
To make her father laugh

I never thought her questions
Would make me scratch my head
But glad I thought to watch each move
And all the things I've said

Who ever thought that fatherhood would
Bring about such pride
And who'd a thought a little girl
Would actually confide

Her day to day discoveries and
All in life she learns
For all the hope I have for her
She's started to affirm

And I can only thank the Lord
For what's been heaven sent
A love so unconditional
I've found makes me content

To move about in life each day
Awaiting that young smile
And rushing home to get that hug
Which makes each day worthwhile.

## The Sum

What is it?
What is it that won't allow me to forget?
Why do I find my thoughts stuck like glue?
Trying my best not to overlook the current status

What's this fascination?
I'm frustrated irritated and somewhat intimidated
I just can't overstand such a curious fixation
Blinded by the light of something that's not quite
a crave
And not quite intrigue
Its something in between

Then, how do I express these expressions and
To whom are they to be expressed?
My head has created the mess

And Thus far I have not been able to escape
Walking away or even running
Not to mention shunning
This notion that accompanies so many of my own
notions
I'm in an ocean of disorder, disruption and
commotion

Because I don't know what it is
What it is that won't allow me to forget
And has my thoughts stuck like glue...
On the sum of you.

## Ode to Wifey

Baby, you are the love of my life see
Grateful you became my wifey
You're my balance; reassurance is what you
provide
Got my nose open wide
I'm excited, cause our love can't be denied

You strengthen me like rays from the sun
You complete me in more ways than one

You're not an open book but
Together we've written many chapters
And I've accepted you as my captor
Then given you my all…
Changed your name to Jones from Walls
And that I don't take lightly
Baby, not even slightly

Don't be confused by what I mean
May seem cliché but you're my queen
And I would take a bullet protecting your flesh
Not because I'm brave like that
But because you keep me fresh
And you've seen that manifest
Through my flow
I'll keep affirming as we grow
Because that's my hearts desire
And I wish I had a choir
To sing the verses of my love for you
Witness that my love accrues
More passion with each tic toc
Baby you are still my rock

See you gave a brother a better life
Stood by through growing pains and strife
Fulfilled my dreams, kept me on point
You made me *sky* just like a joint
And now I'm high as hell on love.
Girl *I know* you're heaven sent from God above.

## For one reason or another

For one reason or another
We seem to have no real control
Especially over where
we end up
So often our hearts yearn for forgotten
relationships
But just as often those relationships,
Too many to mention,
Fail to stand the test of time.

For one reason or another
We find ourselves divided
At times even at the pinnacle
Or greatness of our most cherished friendships
One of the most dificult lessons
For us to learn is that
life's growth spurts
Often creates divisions even from those
we love most.

## King Me

Make me feel like a King!
Not like "Jamie King," the character
Foxx plays in
The comedy situation
And not quite like
The great Reverend Doctor
But more regal like Tut
Or the cartoon-like characters
On playing Cards
Crown me like the tradition
Of checkers calls for
Similar to Arthur of Camelot
But not exactly like that
B.B. the blues man,
CNN's suspender wearer
Or tennis' renowned Billy Jean
Find the gumption to
Recognize and celebrate
My royal reign and
Love me enough to

King Me.

## Place

I'm in that place
That place that makes me feel alone.
The place that's just past the fork in the road, a lil
past frustration.
The place that is always flooded with mixed
feeling and at times is void of fulfillment.
A place right around the corner from being used
and a stone's throw away from throwing in the
towel on overstanding the nonsense.
.

But this place, though it's all the way across town
it sits right up the hill from solitude.

Some say that if you ever reach the pinnacle of
solitude, you'll enjoy beautiful view of Peace of
mind.

Still, I've found myself in the nooks and crannies
of this space, weary of the rat race but eager to
explore new regions like, peace, tranquility and
true morality.

I cannot attempt to explain why I just don't jive
with this turf, I just know that I need to become
too familiar with tranquility.

# I want to go back

I want to go back

To 45's and 8 tracks

To inch worms and big wheels

To being sharp as a tack

I just want to go back


To nose buses and mini bikes

Chinese checkers & fist fights

Back to marbles and jacks

I just need to go back


Back to field days at school

To geranimals and underrooz

To my young uncle smoking "Kools"

To old westerns and pop-lock'n

To pimp walking and slap boxing

I'm going all the way back


To bell bottoms & wide collars

Books of food stamps & silver dollars

To phone booths & rotary phones

To making wishes on wishbones

Can we take this thang back


To hop scotch and jump rope

To English Leather cologne & soap

To word up and that's dope

To racing stripes on gym socks

To Billy Dee & Redd Foxx

I keep trying to go back


Back to football in the streets

To stationwagons w/ third seats

Back to suicide doors

To linoleum floors

I just want to go back

 To a whole lot less drama

To GrandPa and Big Momma

Back to platforms and earthshoes

To services stations and tips too

To monopoly and clue

To you just being you

Click my heels and be back


To the days with less strife

A much simpler life

Back when folks would connect

For pure love and respect

I sit back and reflect

Moments I recollect

And I wish I was back.

## Tribute to Mr. Jackson

Dear Mr. Jackson maybe you don't "Remember
The Time"
That I told you that I needed to find "Another Part
of Me"
Because I was missing that P.Y.T., and we agreed
that I needed
A "Lady In My Life." But you told me to give up
my life as a
"Smooth Criminal" because I no longer needed to
be "Bad!"

I told you to "Beat It" because I was no
"Thriller!"
Your messages seemed "Off the Wall"
But then I thought of your "HIStory" and
overtood that its
"Human Nature" To have "Butterflies" when you
want a "Girlfriend."

So as I began to "Ease on Down" with "Dirty
Diana," who said to Me
"The Way You Make Me Feel" is incredible and
"I want to Rock with You," just as you said she
would.
As I saw life becoming more "Dangerous,"
I eventually found myself At "Heartbreak Hotel"
Trying to become
"Happy" "With A Child's Heart" So I tried to
keep it "In the Closet"
But the "Man in the Mirror" proved to be
"Invincible" and
I couldn't resist the moonwalker in me.

Ultimately, I decided to "Jam," becoming a
"Dancing Machine"
Mind, body, and soul And it must have been my
"Destiny" because to this day, I "Never Can Say
Good Bye"
to rhythms like "Billy Jean" or "Wanna Be Start'n
Someth'n."
Because those songs "Heal The World."

*Thank you Mr. Jackson... RIP 6/25/09*

## I'm Ol school

I'm Ol School, Ol School like Gov' ment Cheese
And showing good manners like "Yes ma'am  and
please"

Ol School like party-line telephones
And watching cartoons like the Flintstones
And others like Hong Kong Fuey
Yeah, I loved Now or Laters, they were yummy
and chewy.
And I waited by the TV to watch the Wonder
Twins,
Not to mention Superman and the Superfriends

I've been Ol School like that NBC Peacock
And that Commercial about verbs, known as
School House Rock!
I'm Ol School; I got extension chord whoop'ns
Sipped orange soda from glass bottles while eat'n
Big Momma's cook'n

Ol school enough to have savored a swallow of
Tang
And I even remember the soulful songs that we
sang (like Marvin)
Because I'm Ol School enough to have given five,
On the Black Hand side and if you gave five too
slow
Wasn't no shame in my game, I *had* to let you
know!

Even then I was Ol School, because I go back like couples skate
And smooth D.J's with deep voices on the radio late.

See I'm Ol School like grade school, the standing broad jump and Free Lunch
Yeah I go back like the Jackson's Cartoon, hot pickles with candy, and the Brady Bunch.

Because just like you...

I'm Ol School.

**Do you remember yours?**

I remember
Biscuits from scratch
Smothered chicken with rice for lunch
The watermelon patch just outside the door
And the cotton-field growing next to it.

I remember the whole house being balanced by
bricks
An old rocking chair in the front room
The tiny old timer's iron often used as a doorstop.
I remember big mahogany bedpost
With mattresses stacked to a higher standard.

That old blue pickup and coffee-can spit-toons
Near the floorboard, near the old rocking chair,
And outside on the big ol' porch.

I remember those little middle size pots
That sat on the uncarpeted hardwood floor of
every bedroom
But never saw the flicker of any stove.

I remember that long dirt road just off the
highway
And that rustic shack in the back and the buzz of
wasps amg hornets

Where folks seem to sneak off to for privacy
Which kept an awful stench.

I remember that my great grandparents
Had gentle, sweet natures and showed us lots of
love
While living a simple life on an old plantation
In a place called Pickens, Arkansas.
Do you remember yours?

### Grandmother Lil'

I can't forget momma; thankful she gave me life
Respect Kim to the fullest, even made her my
wife
Could not mistake K.J. from the day she was born
Though she mirrored a loss that still has my heart
torn

A grandmother's departure from the fold and this
earth
Felt the sting of her impact and the ache of her
worth

She surrendered to winged-ones but left only a
hint
A few heirlooms and quilts that were obviously
meant
To be memoirs of moments that our family spent

With no speedy recovery, she had come to her end
No more call'n her up, no way folks could depend
On the voice of this elder, a grand-motherly-
friend

And I still don't recall how the news was
conveyed
Was aware she was taken by an Angels Brigade

Had the sweetest of hearts though she'd been
through life's brawls
The Matriarch of our family; pure compassion
towards all

Stayed steadfast in God's work, through her

wisdom and truth
Though she comforted seniors often giggled with
youth

I remember so clearly, how she made my soul feel
So with this, I give honor to my Grandmother Lil'.

## Deep In Our Hearts

It was four in the morning when I first got the
call.
Heard my big sister's scream; felt my tears start to
fall.

Was disturbed just to hear of his promise
replaced,
With a family's tragedy that we'd all have to
taste.

Knew that bad news had struck, hated passing it
on.
And through all those emotions I caught
"nephew" and "gone."

So I yelled to the heavens, asking, "how could
this be?"
Knowing, "nephew was sharp to the umpteenth
degree!"

Had a level of focus that would put most to
shame.
An inherited drive very few could proclaim.

With a smile to remember that was bright as the
sun,
And a knack for wisecracks that made verbal
spars fun.

Took a voyage in wartime and performed as he
vowed.

He survived the unthinkable and made us all
proud

He was this family's future; we felt that from the
start.
So forever he'll live through us, deep in our
hearts.


*Dedicated to my nephew and protégé **Christopher
B. Melancon***

## Sister's Ghost

Woke up the other morning before cheese-eggs
and grits.
Awakened to the telephone and momma having
fits.
So my Sister finally did it, slid down that slippery
slope.
A brother from the house of God said Sister is
doing dope.
I knew this day was coming, cause dark deeds
come to light.
Though momma's knees are aching we see no end
in sight.
I've tried and tried to talk to her but Sister won't
come clean.
Her bless-ed heart keeps trying to cope, while
masking she's a fiend.
I know there's no quick fix for this but it's hard to
digest.
I want so much to help someone who hasn't self-
confessed.
She started out just lying, and then she tried to
steal.
Dear Sister cursed her kids so much, that they
may never heal.
Seems, Sisters getting weaker, the kids and house
are gone.
Now everything of value was taken, sold or
pawned.
A powerful concoction man, addicted to a dose.

For every trip to wonderland has summoned
Sister's ghost.


## CANCER


Dazed by world wide venom, its been on the
attack

Variations of an illness that hit hard like that crack

Like a thief in the night, struck-a- many-a-folk

Got us check'n for lumps, plus our brains, lungs,
and throats

Not a being exempt from this treacherous beast

Science stuck on perplexed; haunted by those
deceased

And folks feeble from treatment; off to chemo
again

Millions sparring with CANCER, countless brawl
to the end

For without an exception, CANCER deals out raw
strife

Such a personal tussle, blow for blow for a life

Got folks dawning pink ribbons; Take'n lives in a snap

Snatched my homeboy's mom, Dorothy, Back when we were just chaps

Took my oldest friend, Walker, in the blink of an eye

Left me feeling like science; trying to figure out why

Then it Captured Ms. Lady, never loosened it's grip

Dominoed all her loved ones, cut off life with one snip

So, I'm STOKED when I hear, " the Almighty replaced

The most venomous poison with a merciful grace

For a CANCER SURVIVOR to SURVIVE what they faced

Then remain and live on with the CANCER erased

Only Strength could command such a turn to a twist

For a fighter that fought for the chance to exist

Determination and Courage from a burning desire

Heart and Soul of a Champion for the world
to admire

An ordeal to endure that may never be told

A Survivor's miracle the Almighty controlled.

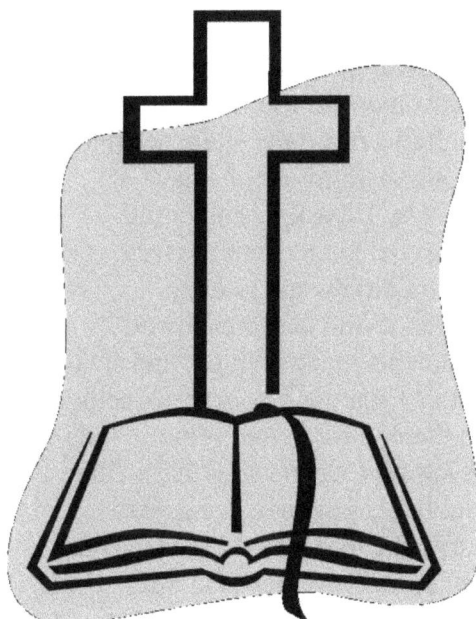

## Peace Be Still

My spirit; peaceful for today
Lawd knows, it's usually not that way
God's grace has helped me overcome
So sacrificing must be done
Like Jesus paying the ultimate cost
That day on Calvary at the cross
No, I'm not saying I'm not still lost
Cause Lawd know I aint ready for preach'n
Just trust me, that too would be reach'n
Though I've heard my share of bible teach'ns
Cannot transform in but a day
That's why I'll ask this as I pray
That I'm delivered from the way
That won't allow me to obey
I know that God deserves my all
Adjustments made both big and small
For He's been there to hear my calls
Been there to catch me from my falls
Lord knows I want a soul that's filled
A soul that's posi-tive-ly healed
The truth be told when un- concealed
I want to feel my Peace Be Still.

## Christmas - Everyone Knows

It's that time of year for family and friends
To celebrate Christmas and how it all began

It happened long ago they say when an Angel
went to Mary
The Angel, Gabriel, spoke for God of a baby she
would carry

He told her that the Holy Spirit would bless her
with a son
Who would also be the Son of God and be known
as the one

To take the name of Jesus Christ, and live on
earth with man
He would heal the sick and raise the dead
 as part of our father's plan.

Now, Mary spoke to Gabriel, when one thing
wasn't quite clear
For she was not yet married then but wanted to
adhere.

The Angel was a messenger, who said, "be not
afraid"
He gave good news from the Lord on high, for
Mary to obey

The Angel, went to Joseph next, and told him in a
dream
That Mary would conceive a child
who would someday rein supreme

So Joseph packed up Mary who had Jesus in her
womb
But after their journey to Bethlehem, the inns
there had no rooms

Mary and Joseph were settled in a stable called a
manger
It was warm and cozy with plenty of straw and
safe from eminent danger

That night, when baby Jesus was born, they
deemed him King of Kings
And wise men traveled from faraway lands, and
gifts for him they did bring

Now, today, we give glory to Jesus Christ, once
rapped in swaddling clothes
So this Christmas Season as you celebrate, make
certain that everyone knows.

## Church Folks

No Sirrrrr brother deacon,
Service ain't moved outside
But a chat with my old friends
Seemed to clash with your old pride

And oh Nawl sister Usher,
From which pew did you come?
With your hand beneath my mouth
Here to confiscate my gum

Why Nawl mother Missionary
I dare not move way up front
I hear perfectly from here
So it's this here seat that I want

And oh no brother Preacher-man
You may think that I have plenty
Can't afford one more dime
Let alone another twenty

Morning Sunday school teacher,
And Yes I recollect
Paying so many dues, having so many rules
But never quite felt much respect.

# Eye

I was thinking of you... funny,
I haven't seen or heard from you
I just wanted you to know that
I am praying for you and
I know that God's eye
is on you too!

## Friday Night Service

Giving honor to God
The Pastor,
First Lady
and the Church mother

Look at your neighbor and say "no ways tired"

Every head Bowed & every eye closed

Testimony 1 through 12

I thank God for blessing me
He's made a way out of no way
He didn't have to do it but he did

An A and a B selection from the youth choir

Tithes and Offering#1,
Offering#2
Offering#3
Building fund

Scriptures

Message

Offering #4 for (whomever brought the message)

Benediction.

**Perfect**

Momma
Always perfect
Even if she tried she could do no wrong
Sweet as pie

Momma born a sinner
But never smoked nothing, drank nothing
Or Stole a thing
like most of the rest of the world.

Momma always said she had never done this sin
or that sin and that she couldn't relate to others
questionable ways.

Momma, resilient, steadfast, unmovable

Momma, a thoroughbred, born with champion's
blood

Momma, the guts of a prizefighter and the heart
and humility of Perfection.

## Only Child

They're a real-life Lifetime movie.
But they're used to it.
She knows that her dad is great,
So she don't let momma's
Poor parenting stress her.
Only annoys her
When her momma comes begg'n for coats,
Cash and other handouts
Because she is her momma's
only child.

## We've Got Baggage Too

Baby we've got baggage too
We've got things and stuff and
Whatchumacalits from Vegas to Kalamazoo


We've got Issues of our own
Which makes us ob-vious-ly prone
To stay lo pro and in our zones
So that the petty things that irk us don't irk you


We too are searching for forever,
Duck and dodge; try'n to be clever,
Just to dig that one enough to call her boo


But since society began
Like you, we've crammed to overstand
Just why the measure of a man is who zooms who


Guess, it's this baggage that we've carried
Just for those worthy adversaries
Who be gaming before game makes its debut


It's not your baggage that we blame
But that week game that some proclaim
By try'n to game another feel'n you do you.

## Just a Jezebel

She was just a Jezebel;
Should have felt it in his heart.

Batting eyes and swinging hips,
Was just the touch to play her part.

Without retreat was no surrender,
But no submission to romance.

And while she flirted, we took notice,
Knowing the brotha had no chance.

The emotion that he showed her
Never built up their rapport.

Cause Jezebel just liked attention
From the brotha she'd ignore.

## Candy for our eyes

We brothas love that sistas are such candy for our
eyes
Like triple chocolate southern ones, a luxury just
to spy
The self-proclaiming plus size ones are down like
two shoe soles
The super-centered- business types stay'n focused
on their goals
The ones that won't give in to love, cause they
were hurt last time
The she's-the-total package ones that we all know
as dimes
The creamy, mahogany, seasoned ones that never
seem to age
The Mohawk wearing risqué ones the spineless
won't engage
The subtle-sexy, loyal, ones, known as the girl
next door
The gangsta-rider-ghetto types; wear'n house
shoes to the store
The sistas dressed in uniforms that work come
rain or shine
The bust- out- all- your- windows ones, that stay
dressed to the nine
The redbone, Cajun, light skinned ones who wear
that trendy gear
The survivors of domestic violence that lived then
persevered

The complicated caramel ones who have such
striking struts
The metropolitan spicy ones who sport those fiery
cuts
The bible carrying amazons that pray for strength
each night
The diva-vein and selfish ones, who have never
been polite
The dreadlocked and the braided ones that give it
to you straight
The this-must-be-my wifey types the ultimate soul
mates
Without regard to color code, with no regard to
size
Without regard to your careers, you brighten up
our lives
And brothas love this medley, such candy for our
eyes.

## She

She was intent on being slippery with words.
An elegant onyx beauty

She, only 30, was as clever as any ones
grandmother,
Had a flare from an unknown origin

She, horribly cautious but addictably mysterious
She, not where I wanted her to be just because I
wanted her to be there

She, not really the bubble gum type but more like
the Farmer's Market kind
She, embracing, thoughtful, tender but selectively
engaging

She an unwilling participant, willing to take
things as far as she wanted.
And She was not perfect, not by a country mile
But my gray skies turned blue when she smiled.

## A Cup of Coffee

The other day they had some words
Let me recap just what occurred.
When she suggested someday soon
They meet for coffee after noon.

No time was set to be exact
Just coffee sipping to relax.
An afternoon to shoot the breeze
To put the butterflies at ease.

He told her weekdays were no good
She followed through; he said she should
But on the week-end called dude up
To see if they could grab a cup.

Instead he blew her off again
Continued that ellusive trend

A cup of coffee proved too much
And had him stuttering and such
To wiggle past that cup of joe
When all he had to say was no.

And still she stalked him as her prey
But all along the dude was gay.

## What The Fuck Happened

What the fuck happened to the good old days
People showing some love minus funny ass ways
And what the fuck happened to just telling the
truth
Why folks lying like rugs when they fail to
produce
Have you spitt'n out venom & wanting knock out
a tooth.

Why are youngsters so angry and show such
disrespect?
Forgotten memories of ancestors being hung by
their necks
And why the fuck do folks feel they can cut a life
short
End up pleading for mercy from them folks up in
court?

And what the fuck happened-to kids going to
school
When we know that without it, they'll end up
being fools,
Have a fifty-fifty chance of living life on a bar
stool.

And what the fuck about family and taking care of
our kin
Now days lazy and shiftless don't get under folks
skin
And taking care of our children, out of wedlock
means squat
Just the right thing to do, so don't act like it's not!

Tell me what the fuck happened to possessing a
skill
Work from dawn until dusk, jobs we've got too
good to fill
And what the fuck happened to being neighbors
and friends
Borrowed sugar and eggs, why the fuck did that
end?

What the fuck ever happened to youth fetching a
switch
Scared to death just to move but not too scared to
snitch
And what the fuck happened to folks paying life's
dues
Thirty days on restriction gave a youngster the
blues

Tell me what the fuck happened to just
swallowing pride
Folks so out of control they've put that to the side
Now we're so unforgiving we won't let nothing
slide

Tell me what the fuck happened to saying yes
ma'am and sir
And what the fuck made us change from the way
we once were!

# B. S.

I've got bad news on good authority
Snap shots of bluez for the majority
I've witnessed youngstas lose their way
Turned into fools, "from gone astray"
Old folks depleted of affection
While youngins bound for State corrections
Complete with tattooed tears & necks
No goals and lack'n self-respect!!!


With unpaid dues, and no employment
But quick to rob folks for enjoyment
Like high-risk heist to quench that thirst
Straight stick-up-kids, who'll snatch a purse
Dropouts without a knowledge base
Who boast and brag of the paper-chase
Like most, I've crammed to overstand
Just when the measure of a man
Changed from his level of advance
To bout' how low he saggs his pants

A shiftless, lazy, villainous crop
With no skill set to want to stop
Bad News from their back porch to yours
Young hoodlums kick'n in front doors
Misguided youth without a care
Won't listen to even an old school player
Old folks aint safe so don't you snooze
Young punks who aint got zip to lose
Our future dazed and so confused
Unsure which avenue to choose


Moms in disgust with blinders on
Won't mention the sad conclusions drawn
Steady cutt'n 'em slack though wayyy off track
But not a peep bout' what Kats really lack
These youngstas drunk and staying high
No drive, No fight, Just gett'n by
Can't front like we don't know the biz
Cause this Smells exactly like what it is!

## Am I my Brother's Keeper?

Am I my brother's Keeper?
When he's sleepy from puff'n on reefer?
When I've taught against sagg'n his pants
Or screwing up what could be his very last chance
To make good on some paramount move
That if executed the right way might possibly
improve

His life's quality while adding dimension
Simultaneously keep'n his ass out of detention
And away from those others, who can talk a good
game
But are shiftless and lazy and aint gone do a damn
thang
And he loves them but what can mere love
accrue?
When you're hungry but won't even do for you?

Should I sit there just holding my peace
Or write verses that rhyme trying to find that
release
Question is will my brother close ranks with his
pride
And learn trade tricks of earning he has not ever
tried

Showed and told him but brother must do as the
rest
Put his nose to the grind and perform I suggest
Sick and tired of the fat that I've had to trim
Saddest part, he's too trifling to do for him
So I ask one mere questions from this verse I've
composed
Spared my dimes for my kin when I know that he
knows?
... But am I my brother's Keeper

## Your Fate Awaits

Are youth so God awful blind
That they 're just stuck here marking time,
Instead of taking place in line,
Where most obtain a chance to shine.

You see, I bow my head in shame
Because these youngsters act insane

97

And then become shiftless and lame
Or go at life without an aim.

Because anyone one could choose
To smoke on blunts or drink on booze.
Instead of walking around confused!
They should be striving to get through.

Yet, they act like life's their foe
So many never seem to grow
Too busy slacking even though
Most don't know what they claim to so...

I have to give it to them straight
Believe the hype you may be great
Fo Sho, your destiny is fate
But paying dues may still await!

## Baffled

I am baffled.

Baffled by the terrible turn that too many young
men have taken.
Struggling, so they beg from us, guess paying
dues has been forsaken.

They fail to be-come disciplined, as stress draws
near, encroaching.
Relying on old failed concepts and still reject
good coaching.

So many that I'm baffled by are throwing away
their lives.
Without regard to legacies or opportunities that
arise.

Accepting jail "without no bail" for using a gun or
knife.
When living by the sword these days' is giving up
ten to life.

It seems to me that our young men retreated from
the fight.
They preconceive their destinies and bought into
scandalous plights.

Now help me understand how showing your
boxer shorts means style.
And why the ones I'm baffled by perceive those
soft that smile.

Some rob and steal and even kill and some just act
like jerks.
They won't enroll in school most times and then
won't go to work.

Most won't take that Mc Donald's job, it's just too
much to ask.
And then they try to parent kids but that's a
tougher task.

With cars that are not registered or on insurance
plans,
But plenty boom to move a room and rims cause
they're "the man."

They're hardly ever sober, cause that's too much
like right.
But when we call them out on this, then they're
prepared to fight.

Some beat up on their women and some don't pay
their bills.
Yet every time you speak to them, they 're talk'n
bout keeping it real.

Why does it have to be this way; we've all been
blessed with gifts
Just try to set a goal or two and the paradigm will
shift.

The time has come for this campaign; A change
from this can't wait!
For if they put this off today tomorrow may be too
late.

## SkelaTONS

I've got skelaTONS in the back of my mind
That need to be addressed
A smorgasbord of demons man
That dare not let me rest
Like when I was just in junior high,
And Acting like a louse
By breaking in the locker rooms
To lift Levi and Straus
True acts of try'n to be a thug
Though I'd been raised in church.
Took nickels from the offering plate
As deacons formed a search

And then I stole my step dad's car,
When I was but a lad
Even rifled through my momma's purse
To swipe the change she had.
And sticking up the pizza man
For doe when I had plenty
A soldier in the Army
Should know better at age twenty
And then I got to college
And was back to rifling purses
The guilt I felt from life bred
Sunday School and Bible verses

I still breakout perspiring
Often waking from my sleep
My delinquent past consumes me
Often causing me to weep

For when I awake in thirst
To find I'm reaching out for water
I pray the seeds I've sown Myself,
I don't reap through my daughter

But what's a man supposed to do to
Move right past his past
Especially when present life
Dictates complete contrast
My feeling is that the smartest folks
Know pasts can just be bruising
So I'll write this now and turn the page
Cause life gets more confusing.

## Yourself Insane

What are you doing now
That seems to help you to get through
Are you packing up your ancient life
To bring about a new
Or- simply- soul-searching
Trying to get in touch with you

Do you pass your time by drinking
When you know you should be thinking
About the watch
You need to watch because
That time frames always shrinking

This life's yours for the picking
Although yours may not be clicking
So be wise enough to see the light
Through hearts and minds conflicting

Twist this around your brain
This world is your domain
So live life with No Worries and
Don't drive yourself insane.

## Part Of Me

This piece is but a part of me
There's so much some may never see
Like the me that I aspire to be
And though there is no guarantee
My goal to let my mind be free
So that I may potentially
Be made a proper designee
I pray that God will hear my plea
Pray that I'm made more like a tree
For growth is good essentially
Hu-mil-ity; must be the key
I'm down upon my knees for thee
Please cleanse my soul of all debris
Propel my world eventually
Lord simply be-come part of me.

## A Legacy Worthwhile

When I am dead and gone from here, and buried
six feet deep,
I wonder if they'll cry for me, I wonder who will
weep.
So many untrue friendships have failed the test of
time.
For loyalty is rare these days, and oh, so hard to
find.
I wonder when my flesh is spoiled If I'll receive
just due.
Or will folks simply gossip, finding pleasure in
my debut.
When heaven opens up it's gates and sounds the
duty horn
And pearly gates light up the sky I wonder if
they'll mourn
An unappreciated man, with scars from such
contempt,
But love for all his fellowmen though some have
proved exempt.
Cause when I think of death most times, I think
how they'll connect
The good and bad I've said or done, and all of its
effects.
One can't ignore these sentiments, for I've been
who I am,
An unapologetic truth until that casket slams.
I've lived my life with discipline; have had but
few regrets,

With systematic principles some view as
clandestine threats.
When time has ticked its last tick tock and my last
seed is sown
I pray for virtues good enough that honor will be
shown.
So when I've said those final words to both my
wife and child
I hope that God will deem my life and legacy
worthwhile.

## Where Have The Poets Gone?

Where have all the poet gone?
Have they all lost their Pens?
No metaphors or similes
Being authored by my friends?


We use to write of love and life
Would jot thoughts down with ease
But seems that they've all disappeared
Turned into absentees


No scribes are here parading works
Can't guess what's on their minds
Must not give in to writer's block
So scribble through that grind


Oh, how I've missed the Poets here
I'll await dramatic returns
Because without their poetry
Surrender breeds concern


I hope to see their works again
I pray they come back soon
For Poets do light up the world
Like sunny afternoons.

## My Mind Defies Odds

My mind
Will not un-wind
Right now, so that I can find
The time.

To tinker with a word or two
And send the world a clue
That some may find an interest in
While others view taboo

Without ideal ideas right now
No calculated flow
I play this game
Exchanging words like Clampants play banjos
Life takes some funny turns & twists

On this we I do rely
But, I take life just as it comes
So odds I may defy.

*In Loving Memory of my mother,*
*Bama Jean Wells*
*September 15, 1944 - June 24, 2017*

## ACKNOWLEDGEMENTS

*I would like to thank my wife Kim and my*
*daughter Kyla for allowing me to create. I realize*
*that my time creating is most often time away*
*from you. Thank you for giving me that time.*

*This book is dedicated to my nephew Christopher*
*Bryce Melancon. May God continue to watch over*
*your loved ones. I give thanks to God for giving*
*me the gift of words. I could not have written*
*these words without his favor.*

*To my best friend, Lou Collins, thanks for being*
*an inspiration, to my brother and SIL, Sabrina,*
*thanks for making love happen again... I love you*
*both... To the circle you know who you are.*
*"Faith without work is dead!"*

*To Theresa Gonsalves, thanks a billion times,*
*you're my shero but this wordsmith has no words.*
*Thank you!*

*To Patricia Hoover, thank you for your much*
*needed expertise "the all-seeing eye." Thank you!*

*To Natasha Hughes your input has been*
*invaluable and you very well may have a future in*
*the literary world (smile). Thank you!*

*To readers all over the world, I hope you find that the* **Poetic Chronicles** *take you on a literary journey. I do appreciate the love and kindness that has been given to me from those that have been able to relate to my words. Please know that I continue to write as my contribution to real life in real time. God Bless YOU world...Keep poetry in motion*

*Jazz Matazz*

FAN CLUB ENTERTAINMENT
PUBLISHING

Contact Info:

Attn: Jeff Jones aka Jazz Matazz
P.O. box 271570
Las Vegas, Nevada 89127

Email: jazzwlv@gmail.com

Ph: 702-349-9213

www.ingramcontent.com/pod-product-compliance
Lightning Source LLC
LaVergne TN
LVHW091159080426
835509LV00006B/751